CARNIVORE

COOKBOOK

"Quick and Crispy Recipes for Meat Lovers"

ALLIE NAGEL

Copyright © 2023 by Allie Nagel

DISCLAIMER

This cookbook is intended to provide general information and recipes.

The recipes provided in this cookbook are not intended to replace or be a substitute for medical advice from a physician.

The reader should consult a healthcare professional for any specific medical advice, diagnosis or treatment.

Any specific dietary advice provided in this cookbook is not intended to replace or be a substitute for medical advice from a physician.

The author is not responsible or liable for any adverse effects experienced by readers of this cookbook as a result of following the recipes or dietary advice provided.

The author makes no representations or warranties of any kind (express or implied) as to the accuracy, completeness, reliability or suitability of the recipes provided in this cookbook.

The author disclaims any and all liability for any damages arising out of the use or misuse of the recipes provided in this cookbook. The reader must also take care to ensure that the recipes provided in this cookbook are prepared and cooked safely.

The recipes provided in this cookbook are for informational purposes only and should not be used as a substitute for professional medical advice, diagnosis or treatment.

TABLE OF CONTENTS

INTRODUCTION 9

CHAPTER 1 11

UNDERSTANDING THE CARNIVORE DIET 11

BENEFITS OF A CARNIVORE DIET 11

FOODS TO EAT DURING CARNIVORE DIET 11

FOODS TO AVOID DURING CARNIVORE DIET ... 13

TIPS AND TRICKS ON HOW TO FOLLOW A CARNIVORE DIET 15

CHAPTER 3 21

14-DAY MEAL PLAN 21

CHAPTER 3 25

40 NUTRITIOUS RECIPES FOR A CARNIVORE DIET 25

BREAKFAST 25

Air-Fried Steak Bites 25

Air-Fried Pork Chops 26

Air-Fried Lamb Chops 27

Air-Fried Salmon Fillets 28

Air-Fried Turkey Sausage Patties 29

LUNCH 30

Air-Fried Ribeye Steak 30

Air-Fried Bacon-Wrapped Chicken Tenders 31

Air-Fried Turkey Wings 32

Rosemary Garlic Air-Fried Duck Breast 33

Air-Fried Shrimp Skewers 35

DINNER 36

Crispy Air-Fried Chicken Thighs 36

Air-Fried Garlic Butter Shrimp: 37

Air-Fried Turkey Legs 38

Air Fryer Beef Kabobs 39

Air-Fried Bison Burgers 40

BEEF 41

Air Fried Beef Burger 41

Air Fried Beef Liver 42

Air Fried Beef Brisket 43

Air Fried Beef Kabobs 44

Air Fried Beef Jerky... 45

POULTRY.. 47

Air-Fried Chicken Wings.................................... 47

Lemon Pepper Air-Fried Chicken Drumsticks............. 48

Buffalo Ranch Air-Fried Quail 49

Paprika and Herb Air-Fried Cornish Hens................... 50

Herb-Crusted Air-Fried Goose Legs.......................... 51

PORK.. 52

Cajun-Spiced Air-Fried Pork Shoulder...................... 54

Mustard and Herb Marinated Air-Fried Pork Loin....... 55

Rosemary and Lemon Air-Fried Pork Medallions........ 56

Paprika and Cumin Crusted Air-Fried Pork Steaks 57

LAMB.. 59

Air-Fried Lamb Burgers....................................... 59

Air-Fried Lamb Meatballs 60

Air-Fried Lamb Kebabs 61

Air-Fried Lamb Steaks.. 62

Air-Fried Lamb Shoulder Chunks 63

SEAFOOD 64

Air-Fried Garlic Butter Lobster Tails 64

Crispy Air-Fried Coconut Shrimp 66

Cajun Air-Fried Catfish 67

Lemon Herb Air-Fried Scallops 68

Herb-Infused Air-Fried Swordfish 69

CONCLUSION 70

INTRODUCTION

The Carnivore Diet is a nutritional strategy that promotes consuming only animal products, mainly meat.

Proponents contend that because humans are carnivores by nature, cutting out plant-based diets can have a number of positive health effects. They assert that the diet encourages weight loss, enhances mental clarity, and helps control blood sugar levels.

The core of the carnivore diet is consuming only animal products, which include meat, fish, eggs, and some dairy products, and avoiding all plant-based foods, which include grains, legumes, fruits, and vegetables.

Experts in nutrition and health have debated this drastic divergence from standard dietary norms.

Proponents of the Carnivore Diet frequently emphasize how it can help with autoimmune diseases and digestive disorders, among other health concerns.

They contend that cutting out plant-based foods lowers inflammation and promotes healthy digestion.

Furthermore, the diet offers vital nutrients in highly accessible forms, implying that animal products give important fatty acids, complete proteins, and a variety of vitamins and minerals.

Critics worry about the Carnivore Diet's possible disadvantages, though.

They highlight the danger of deficiency in certain nutrients, especially those present in plant-based meals like fiber and vitamins. There are concerns over the long-term viability of this kind of restrictive diet as well as its overall health effects.

There is little scientific research on the long-term impact and safety of the Carnivore Diet, despite the prevalence of anecdotal success tales.

People who are thinking about adopting this dietary strategy should proceed with caution and consult medical specialists to make sure they are meeting their nutritional needs and minimizing any hazards that may arise from following such a restrictive eating pattern.

CHAPTER 1

UNDERSTANDING THE CARNIVORE DIET

BENEFITS OF A CARNIVORE DIET

1. Because a carnivore diet increases fat burning and decreases carbohydrate intake, it can be an effective weight loss strategy.

2. Carnivore diets can help stabilize blood sugar levels by removing carbohydrates, which may lessen energy crashes.

3. A carnivore diet's high fat content supplies a steady energy supply, resulting in an increase in general energy levels.

4. A carnivorous diet can help you achieve mental acuity and concentrate. This effect may be brought about by stabilized blood sugar levels and ketosis.

5. Because a meat-based diet eliminates many common irritants, it can be simple you with their digestive problems.

6.   Reducing inflammatory foods from the diet, such as grains and processed sugars, may help the body experience less inflammation.

7.   Eating more nutrients, especially important fatty acids, can help maintain better skin.

8.   Foods high in fat and protein can help control hunger, which may prevent overindulging.

9.   For people who exercise regularly, consuming enough protein helps to maintain and strengthen their muscles.

10. Although individual results vary, some athletes on carnivore diets report increased endurance and performance.

11. For some people, cutting back on inflammatory foods may help improve their joint health.

12. Some users report benefits in illnesses like PCOS or hormone abnormalities, and a carnivorous diet may help support hormonal balance.

13. For some people, better nutrition and stable blood sugar levels might have a good impact on the quality of their sleep.

14. Meal preparation and planning can be made easier by the carnivore diet's simplicity.

15. Although further research is required to definitively confirm these claims, some proponents assert that a carnivore diet can have therapeutic effects on specific illnesses.

FOODS TO EAT DURING CARNIVORE DIET

1. **Red Meat:** An integral part of the carnivore diet, red meat is high in vital minerals such as iron and B vitamins.

2. **Poultry:** Lean protein sources rich in necessary amino acids include chicken and turkey.

3. **Fish:** Omega-3 fatty acids found in fatty fish, such as mackerel and salmon, support heart and brain function.

4. **Eggs:** Packed with nutrients, eggs are an excellent source of protein, good fats, and a variety of vitamins.

5. **Organ Meats:** Rich in vitamins and minerals like iron, zinc, and vitamin A, the liver, kidney, and heart are nutritional powerhouses.

6. **Bacon:** Rich in fat and a tasty complement to meals, bacon is a favorite food among carnivorous dieters.

7. **Bone Marrow:** An essential part of a carnivore's diet, bone marrow is high in collagen and good lipids.

8. **Bone broth:** An electrolyte- and nutrient-rich liquid that promotes general health.

9. **Cheese (if tolerated):** To add variety and extra fat, some carnivores consume specific kinds of cheese.

10. **Pork:** Pork has a variety of cuts that are good sources of protein and healthy fats for the diet.

11. **Lamb:** Lamb is a tasty and nutrient-dense red meat alternative.

12. **Ground beef:** A mainstay for many carnivore aficionados, ground beef is versatile and simple to cook.

13. **Salt:** Although salt isn't a food, it's essential for preserving electrolyte balance, particularly when following a low-carb diet.

14. **Water:** Although it's not a food, drinking enough of it is crucial, particularly when cutting back on carbs, which cause the body to retain water.

FOODS TO AVOID DURING CARNIVORE DIET

1. **Grains:** Because they are heavy in carbs, grains like wheat, rice, and oats are usually not included in a carnivore's diet.

2. **Legumes:** Some persons on a carnivorous diet would want to avoid the lectins and phytates found in beans, lentils, and peas.

3. **Vegetables:** The carnivore diet excludes the majority of vegetables because they are high in carbohydrates. This covers cruciferous veggies, root vegetables, and leafy greens.

4. **Fruits:** Since a carnivore diet tries to reduce the amount of carbohydrates consumed, fruits are typically avoided due to their high sugar content.

5. **Processed Foods:** Strict carnivore diets shouldn't include processed foods because they frequently include sweets, preservatives, and additives.

6. **Sugars & Sweeteners:** Both natural and artificial sweeteners are included since they raise blood sugar levels and increase the consumption of carbohydrates.

7. **Dairy (for some):** Although some carnivores eat dairy, some don't because they may be lactose intolerant or because they are worried about particular proteins.

8. **Nuts and seeds:** Their high carbohydrate and anti-nutrient content makes them off limits.

9. Vegetable Oils: Avoid vegetable oils in favor of animal fats because they are high in omega-6 fatty acids, such as soybean, canola, and maize oil.

10. **Processed Meats with Additives:** Certain processed meats are not ideal for a strict carnivore diet since they may contain sugars, fillers, or other additives.

11. **Highly Processed Snacks:** Because of their high carbohydrate and frequently inflammatory content, chips, crackers, and other snack foods are generally avoided.

12. **Alcohol:** Due to their sugar content and potential to disrupt ketosis, alcoholic beverages are not allowed.

13. **Coffee (and tea):** Although these beverages are frequently ingested during a carnivorous diet, some people prefer not to take caffeine.

14. **Artificial Additives:** To preserve a natural and less processed approach, preservatives, colorings, and flavorings—found in many processed foods—are removed.

15. **Soy-Based Products:** Because soy includes phytoestrogens and anti-nutrients, some practitioners of carnivore diets avoid consuming it.

TIPS AND TRICKS ON HOW TO FOLLOW A CARNIVORE DIET

1. **Educate Yourself:** Understand the principles of the carnivore diet, its benefits, and potential challenges before starting.

2. **Plan Your Meals:** Preparing carnivore-friendly meals in advance can help you stick to the diet and avoid temptations.

3. **Hydrate:** Drink plenty of water to stay hydrated, especially as a low-carb diet can lead to increased water loss.

4. **Include Variety:** While the diet is primarily meat-based, try to include a variety of meats, organ meats, and fats to ensure a broader nutrient intake.

5. **Monitor Electrolytes:** Maintain proper electrolyte balance by adding salt to your meals and considering magnesium and potassium supplements if needed.

6. **Listen to Your Body:** Pay attention to how your body responds to the diet, and adjust based on

your energy levels, cravings, and overall well-being.

7. **Intermittent Fasting:** Consider incorporating intermittent fasting to enhance fat burning and promote ketosis.

8. **Choose Quality Meats:** Opt for grass-fed and pasture-raised meats, when possible, as they may offer additional nutritional benefits.

9. **Include Fatty Cuts:** Embrace fatty cuts of meat for sustained energy and satiety.

10. **Be Mindful of Protein Intake:** While protein is essential, excessive protein intake can be counterproductive. Adjust your protein intake based on your individual needs.

11. **Avoid Sneaky Carbs:** Be vigilant about hidden carbs in processed meats or seasonings, which could unintentionally affect your carb intake.

12. **Supplement Wisely:** If necessary, consider supplements for nutrients not adequately obtained through your diet, such as vitamin D or omega-3 fatty acids.

13. **Manage Transition Period:** Be aware of potential side effects during the adaptation phase, commonly known as the "carnivore flu," and be patient as your body adjusts.

14. **Connect with Others:** Join online communities or forums to share experiences, tips, and advice with fellow carnivore practitioners.

15. **Regular Health Check-ups:** Regularly monitor your health with blood tests and consult with a healthcare professional to ensure nutritional adequacy and overall well-being.

CHAPTER 3

14-DAY MEAL PLAN

DAY 1

Breakfast: Air-Fried Steak Bites

Lunch: Air-Fried Ribeye Steak

Dinner: Crispy Air-Fried Chicken Thighs

DAY 2

Breakfast: Air-Fried Pork Chops

Lunch: Air-Fried Bacon-Wrapped Chicken Tenders

Dinner: Air-Fried Garlic Butter Shrimp:

DAY 3

Breakfast: Air-Fried Lamb Chops

Lunch: Air-Fried Turkey Wings

Dinner: Air-Fried Turkey Legs

DAY 4

Breakfast: Air-Fried Salmon Fillets

Lunch: Rosemary Garlic Air-Fried Duck Breast

Dinner: Air Fryer Beef Kabobs

DAY 5

Breakfast: Air-Fried Turkey Sausage Patties

Lunch: Air-Fried Shrimp Skewers

Dinner: Air-Fried Bison Burgers

DAY 6

Breakfast: Air Fried Beef Burger

Lunch: Air-Fried Chicken Wings

Dinner: Air-Fried Lamb Burgers

DAY 7

Breakfast: Air Fried Beef Liver

Lunch: Lemon Pepper Air-Fried Chicken Drumsticks

Dinner: Air-Fried Lamb Meatballs

DAY 8

Breakfast: Air Fried Beef Brisket

Lunch: Buffalo Ranch Air-Fried Quail

Dinner: Air-Fried Lamb Kebabs

DAY 9

Breakfast: Air Fried Beef Kabobs

Lunch: Paprika and Herb Air-Fried Cornish Hens

Dinner: Air-Fried Lamb Steaks

DAY 10

Breakfast: Air Fried Beef Jerky

Lunch: Herb-Crusted Air-Fried Goose Legs

Dinner: Air-Fried Lamb Shoulder Chunks

DAY 11

Breakfast: Air-Fried Steak Bites

Lunch: Air-Fried Ribeye Steak

Dinner: Crispy Air-Fried Chicken Thighs

DAY 12

Breakfast: Air-Fried Pork Chops

Lunch: Air-Fried Bacon-Wrapped Chicken Tenders

Dinner: Air-Fried Garlic Butter Shrimp:

DAY 13

Breakfast: Air-Fried Lamb Chops

Lunch: Air-Fried Turkey Wings

Dinner: Air-Fried Turkey Legs

DAY 14

Breakfast: Air-Fried Salmon Fillets

Lunch: Rosemary Garlic Air-Fried Duck Breast

Dinner: Air Fryer Beef Kabobs

CHAPTER 3

40 NUTRITIOUS RECIPES FOR A CARNIVORE DIET

BREAKFAST

Air-Fried Steak Bites

Preparation Time: 20 Minutes

Serves: 4

Calories: 250

Ingredients:

1 lb. steak, preferably ribeye or sirloin, cut into bite-sized pieces

Salt and pepper, to taste

Optional: garlic powder or other preferred seasonings

Method of Preparation:

1. Season the steak bites with salt, pepper, and any optional seasonings, ensuring they are evenly coated.
2. Preheat the air fryer to 400°F (200°C).

3. Place the seasoned steak bites in a single layer in the air fryer basket, ensuring they are not overcrowded.

4. Air fry for 8-10 minutes, flipping the steak bites halfway through, or until they reach your desired level of doneness.

5. Remove from the air fryer, let them rest for a few minutes, and serve.

Air-Fried Pork Chops

Preparation Time: 30 Minutes

Serves: 4

Calories: 300

Ingredients:

4 pork chops

Salt and pepper, to taste

Optional: paprika or other preferred seasonings

Method of Preparation:

1. Season the pork chops with salt, pepper, and any optional seasonings, ensuring they are evenly coated.

2. Preheat the air fryer to 380°F (190°C).

3. Place the seasoned pork chops in a single layer in the air fryer basket.

4. Air fry for 12-15 minutes, flipping halfway through, or until the internal temperature reaches at least 145°F (63°C).

5. Allow the pork chops to rest for a few minutes before serving.

Air-Fried Lamb Chops

Preparation Time: 35 Minutes

Serves: 4

Calories: 350

Ingredients:

8 lamb chops

Salt and pepper, to taste

Optional: rosemary or other preferred seasonings

Method of Preparation:

1. Season the lamb chops with salt, pepper, and any optional seasonings, ensuring they are evenly coated.
2. Preheat the air fryer to 400°F (200°C).
3. Place the seasoned lamb chops in a single layer in the air fryer basket.
4. Air fry for 10-12 minutes, flipping halfway through, or until the internal temperature reaches your desired level of doneness.
5. Allow the lamb chops to rest for a few minutes before serving.

Air-Fried Salmon Fillets

Preparation Time: 15 minutes

Serves: 2

Calories: 350

Ingredients:

Fresh Salmon Fillets

Salt

Pepper

Olive Oil

Method of Preparation:

1. Preheat the air fryer to 400°F (200°C).
2. Pat the salmon fillets dry and season with salt and pepper.
3. Brush olive oil over the fillets for a crispy texture.
4. Place the fillets in the air fryer basket, ensuring they are not overcrowded.
5. Air fry for 10-12 minutes, flipping halfway through, until the salmon is cooked to your desired doneness.

Air-Fried Turkey Sausage Patties

Preparation Time: 20 minutes

Serves: 4

Calories: 400

Ingredients:

Ground Turkey

Salt

Pepper

Garlic Powder

Method of Preparation:

1. Preheat the air fryer to 375°F (190°C).
2. Mix ground turkey with salt, pepper, and garlic powder to taste.
3. Shape the seasoned turkey mixture into patties.
4. Place the patties in the air fryer basket, ensuring they are not touching.
5. Air fry for 10-15 minutes, flipping halfway through, until the patties are golden brown and reach an internal temperature of 165°F (74°C).

LUNCH

Air-Fried Ribeye Steak

Preparation Time: 15 minutes

Serves: 1

Calories: 150

Ingredients:

Ribeye Steak

Salt

Pepper

Olive Oil

Method of Preparation:

1. Preheat the air fryer to 400°F (200°C).
2. Season the ribeye steak with salt and pepper on both sides.
3. Brush olive oil over the steak for added flavor and a crispy exterior.
4. Place the steak in the air fryer basket, ensuring it's not overcrowded.
5. Air fry for 10-12 minutes, flipping halfway through for medium-rare. Adjust time for desired doneness.

Air-Fried Bacon-Wrapped Chicken Tenders

Preparation Time: 25 minutes

Serves: 2

Calories: 150

Ingredients:

Chicken Tenders

Bacon Strips

Salt

Pepper

Paprika (optional)

Method of Preparation:

1. Preheat the air fryer to 375°F (190°C).
2. Season chicken tenders with salt, pepper, and paprika if desired.
3. Wrap each chicken tender with a strip of bacon.
4. Place the bacon-wrapped tenders in the air fryer basket, ensuring they are not touching.
5. Air fry for 15-20 minutes until the bacon is crispy and chicken is cooked through.

Air-Fried Turkey Wings

Preparation Time: 45 minutes

Serves: 4

Calories: 350

Ingredients:

Turkey Wings

Salt

Pepper

Garlic Powder

Method of Preparation:

1. Preheat the air fryer to 375°F (190°C).
2. Season turkey wings with salt, pepper, and garlic powder.
3. Place the seasoned turkey wings in the air fryer basket, ensuring they are not overlapping.
4. Air fry for 30-40 minutes, flipping halfway through, until wings are golden and reach an internal temperature of 165°F (74°C).

Rosemary Garlic Air-Fried Duck Breast

Preparation Time: 30 minutes

Serves: 2

Calories: 120

Ingredients:

Duck Breast

Rosemary (dried or fresh)

Garlic Powder

Salt

Pepper

Method of Preparation:

1. Preheat the air fryer to 375°F (190°C).
2. Score the skin of the duck breast and season with salt, pepper, garlic powder, and rosemary.
3. Place the duck breast in the air fryer basket, skin side down.
4. Air fry for 12-15 minutes, then flip and air fry for an additional 10-12 minutes until the skin is crispy and the duck is cooked to your liking.

Air-Fried Shrimp Skewers

Preparation Time: 20 minutes

Serves: 2

Calories: 150

Ingredients:

Shrimp (peeled and deveined)

Olive Oil

Paprika

Garlic Powder

Salt

Pepper

Lemon wedges for serving (optional)

Method of Preparation:

1. Preheat the air fryer to 375°F (190°C).
2. In a bowl, toss shrimp with olive oil, paprika, garlic powder, salt, and pepper.
3. Thread seasoned shrimp onto skewers.

4. Place shrimp skewers in the air fryer basket, ensuring they are not touching.

5. Air fry for 8-10 minutes, turning halfway through, until the shrimp are pink and opaque.

DINNER

Crispy Air-Fried Chicken Thighs

Preparation Time: 35 minutes

Serves: 4

Calories: 300

Ingredients:

Chicken Thighs (bone-in, skin-on)

Salt

Pepper

Paprika (optional)

Olive Oil

Method of Preparation:

1. Preheat the air fryer to 400°F (200°C).

2. Pat chicken thighs dry and season with salt, pepper, paprika (if using), and optional garlic powder.
3. Lightly brush olive oil over the chicken thighs for extra crispiness.
4. Place the chicken thighs in the air fryer basket, ensuring they are not crowded.
5. Air fry for 25-30 minutes, flipping halfway through, until the skin is crispy and the internal temperature reaches 165°F (74°C).

Air-Fried Garlic Butter Shrimp

Preparation Time: 15 minutes

Serves: 2

Calories: 250

Ingredients:

Shrimp (peeled and deveined)

Salt

Pepper

Garlic Powder

Butter (melted)

Method of Preparation:

1. Preheat the air fryer to 375°F (190°C).
2. In a bowl, toss shrimp with salt, pepper, and garlic powder.
3. Place seasoned shrimp in the air fryer basket.
4. Drizzle melted butter over the shrimp.
5. Air fry for 8-10 minutes, shaking the basket halfway through, until the shrimp are pink and cooked through.

Air-Fried Turkey Legs

Preparation Time: 50 minutes

Serves: 2

Calories: 300

Ingredients:

Turkey Legs

Salt

Pepper

Paprika (optional)

Method of Preparation:

1. Preheat the air fryer to 375°F (190°C).
2. Season turkey legs with salt, pepper, and paprika if desired.
3. Place the seasoned turkey legs in the air fryer basket, ensuring they are not touching.
4. Air fry for 40-45 minutes, turning halfway through, until the turkey legs are golden and reach an internal temperature of 165°F (74°C).

Air Fryer Beef Kabobs

Preparation Time: 25 minutes

Serves: 2

Calories: 150

Ingredients:

Beef cubes (sirloin or ribeye)

Salt

Pepper

Garlic Powder

Olive Oil

Method of Preparation:

1. Preheat the air fryer to 375°F (190°C).
2. Season beef cubes with salt, pepper, and garlic powder.
3. Thread the seasoned beef cubes onto skewers.
4. Lightly brush olive oil over the beef kabobs.
5. Place the kabobs in the air fryer basket, ensuring they are not touching.
6. Air fry for 12-15 minutes, turning halfway through, until the beef is cooked to your desired level.

Air-Fried Bison Burgers

Preparation Time: 20 minutes

Serves: 2

Calories: 200

Ingredients:

Ground Bison

Salt

Pepper

Garlic Powder

Method of Preparation:

1. Preheat the air fryer to 375°F (190°C).
2. Season ground bison with salt, pepper, and garlic powder.
3. Shape the seasoned bison into burger patties.
4. Place the bison burgers in the air fryer basket, ensuring they are not touching.
5. Air fry for 10-12 minutes, flipping halfway through, until the burgers reach your preferred level of doneness.

BEEF

Air Fried Beef Burger

Preparation Time: 15 minutes

Serves: 2

Calories: 300

Ingredients:

Ground Beef

Salt

Pepper

Garlic Powder (optional)

Method of Preparation:

1. Preheat the air fryer to 375°F (190°C).
2. Season the ground beef with salt, pepper, and garlic powder if desired.
3. Shape the seasoned beef into burger patties.
4. Place the burger patties in the air fryer basket, ensuring they are not touching.
5. Air fry for 10-12 minutes, flipping halfway through, until the burgers reach your preferred level of doneness.

Air Fried Beef Liver

Preparation Time: 10 minutes

Serves: 2

Calories: 300

Ingredients:

Beef Liver slices

Salt

Pepper

Onion Powder (optional)

Method of Preparation:

1. Preheat the air fryer to 375°F (190°C).
2. Season beef liver slices with salt, pepper, and onion powder if desired.
3. Place the seasoned beef liver slices in the air fryer basket.
4. Air fry for 6-8 minutes, flipping halfway through, until the beef liver is cooked to your liking.

Air Fried Beef Brisket

Preparation Time: 20 minutes

Serves: 2

Calories: 350

Ingredients:

Beef Brisket slices

Salt

Pepper

Garlic Powder

Paprika (optional)

Method of Preparation:

1. Preheat the air fryer to 375°F (190°C).
2. Season beef brisket slices with salt, pepper, garlic powder, and paprika if desired.
3. Place the seasoned beef brisket slices in the air fryer basket.
4. Air fry for 12-15 minutes, flipping halfway through, until the beef brisket is cooked to your desired level.

Air Fried Beef Kabobs

Preparation Time: 25 minutes

Serves: 1

Calories: 250

Ingredients:

Beef cubes (sirloin or ribeye)

Salt

Pepper

Garlic Powder

Olive Oil

Method of Preparation:

1. Preheat the air fryer to 375°F (190°C).
2. Season beef cubes with salt, pepper, and garlic powder.
3. Thread the seasoned beef cubes onto skewers.
4. Lightly brush olive oil over the beef kabobs.
5. Place the kabobs in the air fryer basket, ensuring they are not touching.
6. Air fry for 12-15 minutes, turning halfway through, until the beef is cooked to your desired level.

Air Fried Beef Jerky

Preparation Time: 2-3 hours

Serves: 2

Calories: 300

Ingredients:

Beef strips (thinly sliced)

Salt

Pepper

Garlic Powder

Liquid Smoke (optional)

Method of Preparation:

1. Preheat the air fryer to 160°F (71°C) if possible.
2. Season beef strips with salt, pepper, garlic powder, and optional liquid smoke.
3. Place the seasoned beef strips in the air fryer basket, ensuring they are not touching.
4. Air fry for 2-3 hours, checking and flipping the beef strips every 30 minutes until they reach your desired level of dryness.

POULTRY

Air-Fried Chicken Wings

Preparation Time: 35 minutes

Serves: 2

Calories: 400

Ingredients:

Chicken Wings

Salt

Pepper

Garlic Powder

Baking Powder (optional, for crispiness)

Method of Preparation:

1. Preheat the air fryer to 400°F (200°C).
2. Season chicken wings with salt, pepper, and garlic powder.
3. Optionally, coat wings with baking powder for added crispiness.

4. Place the chicken wings in the air fryer basket, ensuring they are not overcrowded.

5. Air fry for 25-30 minutes, shaking the basket halfway through, until the wings are golden and crispy.

Lemon Pepper Air-Fried Chicken Drumsticks

Preparation Time: 40 minutes

Serves: 2

Calories: 450

Ingredients:

Chicken Drumsticks

Lemon Zest

Pepper

Salt

Olive Oil

Method of Preparation:

1. Preheat the air fryer to 375°F (190°C).
2. Season chicken drumsticks with lemon zest, pepper, salt, and olive oil.
3. Place the seasoned chicken drumsticks in the air fryer basket.
4. Air fry for 30-35 minutes, turning halfway through, until the drumsticks are cooked through and have a golden exterior.

Buffalo Ranch Air-Fried Quail

Preparation Time: 30 minutes

Serves: 2

Calories: 350

Ingredients:

Quail (whole or halved)

Buffalo Sauce

Ranch Seasoning

Salt

Pepper

Method of Preparation:

1. Preheat the air fryer to 375°F (190°C).
2. Season quail with salt, pepper, and a mixture of buffalo sauce and ranch seasoning.
3. Place the seasoned quail in the air fryer basket.
4. Air fry for 15-20 minutes, turning halfway through, until the quail is cooked through and has a flavorful coating.

Paprika and Herb Air-Fried Cornish Hens

Preparation Time: 50 minutes

Serves: 2

Calories: 300

Ingredients:

Cornish Hens

Paprika

Dried Herbs (rosemary, thyme, oregano)

Salt

Pepper

Olive Oil

Method of Preparation:

1. Preheat the air fryer to 375°F (190°C).
2. Season Cornish hens with paprika, dried herbs, salt, pepper, and olive oil.
3. Place the seasoned Cornish hens in the air fryer basket.
4. Air fry for 40-45 minutes, turning halfway through, until the hens are golden brown and reach an internal temperature of 165°F (74°C).

Herb-Crusted Air-Fried Goose Legs

Preparation Time: 55 minutes

Serves: 2

Calories: 350

Ingredients:

Goose Legs

Dried Herbs (rosemary, thyme, oregano)

Salt

Pepper

Olive Oil

Method of Preparation:

1. Preheat the air fryer to 375°F (190°C).
2. Season goose legs with dried herbs, salt, pepper, and olive oil.
3. Place the seasoned goose legs in the air fryer basket.
4. Air fry for 45-50 minutes, turning halfway through, until the goose legs are crispy and cooked through.

PORK

Preparation Time: 45 minutes

Serves: 2

Calories: 200

Ingredients:

Pork Ribs

Salt

Pepper

Paprika

Garlic Powder

Onion Powder

Method of Preparation:

1. Preheat the air fryer to 375°F (190°C).
2. Season pork ribs with salt, pepper, paprika, garlic powder, and onion powder.
3. Place the seasoned pork ribs in the air fryer basket, ensuring they are not overcrowded.
4. Air fry for 30-35 minutes, turning halfway through, until the ribs are crispy and cooked to your liking.

Cajun-Spiced Air-Fried Pork Shoulder

Preparation Time: 35 minutes

Serves: 2

Calories: 250

Ingredients:

Pork Shoulder slices

Cajun Seasoning

Salt

Pepper

Olive Oil

Method of Preparation:

1. Preheat the air fryer to 375°F (190°C).
2. Rub Cajun seasoning, salt, and pepper over pork shoulder slices.
3. Lightly brush olive oil over the pork shoulder.
4. Place the seasoned pork shoulder slices in the air fryer basket.

5. Air fry for 25-30 minutes, turning halfway through, until the pork is cooked and has a crispy exterior.

Mustard and Herb Marinated Air-Fried Pork Loin

Preparation Time: 30 minutes (including marination)

Serves: 2

Calories: 200

Ingredients:

Pork Loin slices

Dijon Mustard

Rosemary (dried or fresh)

Thyme (dried or fresh)

Salt

Pepper

Method of Preparation:

1. Preheat the air fryer to 375°F (190°C).

2. In a bowl, mix Dijon mustard, rosemary, thyme, salt, and pepper to create a marinade.

3. Coat pork loin slices with the mustard and herb marinade.

4. Place the marinated pork loin slices in the air fryer basket.

5. Air fry for 20-25 minutes, turning halfway through, until the pork loin is cooked through.

Rosemary and Lemon Air-Fried Pork Medallions

Preparation Time: 30 minutes (including marination)

Serves: 2

Calories: 278

Ingredients:

Pork Tenderloin

Rosemary (dried or fresh)

Lemon Zest

Salt

Pepper

Olive Oil

Method of Preparation:

1. Preheat the air fryer to 375°F (190°C).
2. Cut pork tenderloin into medallions.
3. In a bowl, mix rosemary, lemon zest, salt, pepper, and olive oil to create a marinade.
4. Coat pork medallions with the rosemary and lemon marinade.
5. Place the marinated pork medallions in the air fryer basket.
6. Air fry for 15-20 minutes, turning halfway through, until the pork is cooked through.

Paprika and Cumin Crusted Air-Fried Pork Steaks

Preparation Time: 30 minutes

Serves: 2

Calories: 250

Ingredients:

Pork Steaks

Paprika

Cumin

Salt

Pepper

Method of Preparation:

1.   Preheat the air fryer to 375°F (190°C).
2.   Season pork steaks with paprika, cumin, salt, and pepper.
3.   Place the seasoned pork steaks in the air fryer basket.
4.   Air fry for 20-25 minutes, turning halfway through, until the pork steaks are cooked through and have a crispy crust.

LAMB

Air-Fried Lamb Burgers

Preparation Time: 20 minutes

Serves: 2

Calories: 400

Ingredients:

Ground Lamb

Salt

Pepper

Garlic Powder

Cumin (optional)

Method of Preparation:

1. Preheat the air fryer to 375°F (190°C).
2. In a bowl, mix ground lamb with salt, pepper, garlic powder, and optional cumin.
3. Shape the seasoned lamb mixture into burger patties.

4. Place the lamb burgers in the air fryer basket.

5. Air fry for 12-15 minutes, turning halfway through, until the burgers reach your preferred level of doneness.

Air-Fried Lamb Meatballs

Preparation Time: 25 minutes

Serves: 2

Calories: 390

Ingredients:

Ground Lamb

Salt

Pepper

Rosemary (dried or fresh)

Olive Oil

Method of Preparation:

1. Preheat the air fryer to 375°F (190°C).

2. In a bowl, mix ground lamb with salt, pepper, and rosemary.

3. Shape the seasoned lamb mixture into meatballs.

4. Lightly brush olive oil over the lamb meatballs.

5. Place the meatballs in the air fryer basket.

6. Air fry for 15-18 minutes, turning halfway through, until the meatballs are cooked through and browned.

Air-Fried Lamb Kebabs

Preparation Time: 25 minutes

Serves: 2

Calories: 350

Ingredients:

Lamb cubes

Salt

Pepper

Paprika

Olive Oil

Method of Preparation:

1. Preheat the air fryer to 375°F (190°C).

2. Season lamb cubes with salt, pepper, paprika, and olive oil.

3. Thread the seasoned lamb cubes onto skewers to make kebabs.

4. Place the lamb kebabs in the air fryer basket.

5. Air fry for 15-20 minutes, turning halfway through, until the kebabs are cooked to your desired level.

Air-Fried Lamb Steaks

Preparation Time: 25 minutes

Serves: 2

Calories: 300

Ingredients:

Lamb Steaks

Salt

Pepper

Garlic Powder

Rosemary (dried or fresh)

Olive Oil

Method of Preparation:

1. Preheat the air fryer to 375°F (190°C).
2. Season lamb steaks with salt, pepper, garlic powder, and rosemary.
3. Lightly brush olive oil over the lamb steaks.
4. Place the seasoned lamb steaks in the air fryer basket.
5. Air fry for 15-20 minutes, turning halfway through, until the lamb steaks are cooked to your liking.

Air-Fried Lamb Shoulder Chunks

Preparation Time: 30 minutes

Serves: 2

Calories: 298

Ingredients:

Lamb Shoulder Chunks

Salt

Pepper

Cumin (optional)

Olive Oil

Method of Preparation:

1. Preheat the air fryer to 375°F (190°C).

2. Season lamb shoulder chunks with salt, pepper, and optional cumin.

3. Lightly brush olive oil over the lamb shoulder chunks.

4. Place the seasoned lamb chunks in the air fryer basket.

5. Air fry for 20-25 minutes, turning halfway through, until the lamb chunks are browned and cooked through.

SEAFOOD

Air-Fried Garlic Butter Lobster Tails

Preparation Time: 15 minutes

Serves: 2

Calories: 198

Ingredients:

Lobster Tails

Butter

Garlic Powder

Salt

Pepper

Lemon (optional)

Method of Preparation:

1. Preheat the air fryer to 375°F (190°C).
2. Split lobster tails in half lengthwise.
3. In a bowl, melt butter and mix with garlic powder, salt, and pepper.
4. Brush the garlic butter mixture over the lobster tails.
5. Place the lobster tails in the air fryer basket.
6. Air fry for 8-10 minutes until the lobster is opaque and cooked through.

7.   Optionally, squeeze lemon over the lobster tails before serving.

Crispy Air-Fried Coconut Shrimp

Preparation Time: 20 minutes

Serves: 2

Calories: 250

Ingredients:

Shrimp (peeled and deveined)

Coconut Flour

Eggs (beaten)

Shredded Coconut

Salt

Pepper

Method of Preparation:

1.   Preheat the air fryer to 375°F (190°C).

2.   Dredge shrimp in coconut flour, dip in beaten eggs, and coat with shredded coconut.

3.   Place the coated shrimp in the air fryer basket, ensuring they are not touching.

4.   Air fry for 8-10 minutes, turning halfway through, until the coconut shrimp are golden and crispy.

Cajun Air-Fried Catfish

Preparation Time: 25 minutes

Serves: 2

Calories: 200

Ingredients:

Catfish Fillets

Cajun Seasoning

Salt

Pepper

Olive Oil

Method of Preparation:

1.   Preheat the air fryer to 375°F (190°C).

2. Season catfish fillets with Cajun seasoning, salt, and pepper.

3. Lightly brush olive oil over the catfish fillets.

4. Place the seasoned catfish fillets in the air fryer basket.

5. Air fry for 12-15 minutes, turning halfway through, until the catfish is cooked and has a crispy exterior.

Lemon Herb Air-Fried Scallops

Preparation Time: 15 minutes

Serves: 2

Calories: 190

Ingredients:

Scallops

Lemon Zest

Dried Herbs (rosemary, thyme)

Salt

Pepper

Olive Oil

Method of Preparation:

1. Preheat the air fryer to 375°F (190°C).

2. Pat dry scallops with paper towels to remove excess moisture.

3. In a bowl, mix lemon zest, dried herbs, salt, pepper, and olive oil.

4. Coat scallops with the herb mixture.

5. Place the seasoned scallops in the air fryer basket, ensuring they are not touching.

6. Air fry for 6-8 minutes until the scallops are opaque and have a golden crust.

Herb-Infused Air-Fried Swordfish

Preparation Time: 20 minutes

Serves: 2

Calories: 200

Ingredients:

Swordfish Steaks

Dried Herbs (thyme, oregano)

Salt

Pepper

Olive Oil

Method of Preparation:

1. Preheat the air fryer to 375°F (190°C).

2. Season swordfish steaks with dried herbs, salt, pepper, and olive oil.

3. Place the seasoned swordfish steaks in the air fryer basket.

4. Air fry for 12-15 minutes, turning halfway through, until the swordfish is cooked and has a flavorful crust.

CONCLUSION

Ultimately, the carnivore diet in this book is not only tasty, it is a way of life, a way to reconnect with the essence of food, and a way to get back to your ancestral origins.

You must have discovered the amazing adaptability of products derived from animals during this culinary journey, demonstrating that a meat-based diet does not have to be boring.

Every recipe, from flavorful chops to tender steaks, offers a symphony of flavors that satisfy the body's nutritional requirements while simultaneously teasing the palate.

As explained in this book, the carnivore diet is proof that using basic foods may provide rich flavors and health advantages.

The carnivore diet offers several possible health benefits, such as increased energy and mental clarity, beyond just enjoying delicious food. You can reassess your connection with food and see directly the significant impact it can have on your health by adopting this dietary philosophy.

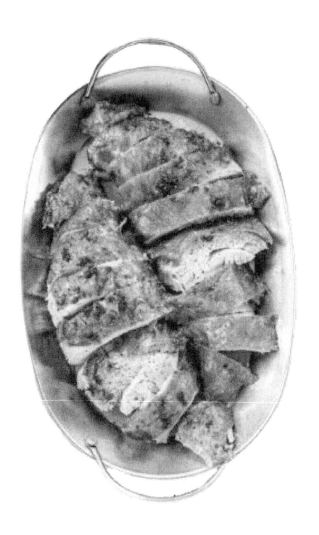

Printed in Great Britain
by Amazon

37079257R00046